Off the Beaten Path

Discovering Powell River and the Upper Sunshine Coast

Published by JCJ Holdings Ltd.
7080 Tofino Street, Powell River, BC Canada V8A 1G3
Tel: 604-485-0824
Website: www.bcphotobooks.ca
Email: jcjholdings@shaw.ca

Editing, Layout and Design by Emma Levez Larocque
Sales and Marketing by Tara Chernoff
Maps and Artwork by Abby-Gail J. Hyldig
Photographs by Emma Levez Larocque, except: "Pacific White-Sided Dolphin" and "Texada Island (Marble Bay)" by Lorrie Pirart; "Music" and "Nun Kum Dancers," courtesy of the Powell River Academy of Music; and "Scuba Diving" by Parris Champoise
Proofreading (all) by Tara Chernoff, Matt Larocque, Will Chernoff
Proofreading (select pieces) by Teedie Kagume, Kate Spanks, Susan Biagi, Kate Saunders, John A. Campbell, Erik Blaney, Terry Sabine, Russell Storry, Adam Vallance, Lorrie Pirart, Sandra Phillips, Daryl Smith, Janet Falk, Marie Claxton, Eagle Walz, Diana Wood, Parris Champoise, and John Ford.
Research Assistance by Teedie Kagume of the Powell River Historical Museum
Resources: *Texada Island* by Bill Thompson; *Hulks: The Breakwater Ships of Powell River* by John A. Campbell; *Sunshine & Salt Air: Sunshine Coast Recreation & Visitors Guide*, edited by Peter A. Robson; *Powell River's First 50 Years* published by A.H. Alsgard; *Pacific Coast* by Bayard H. McConnaughey and Evelyn McConnaughey; *Against Wind & Weather: The History of Towboating in British Columbia* by Ken Drushka; *Golf in Powell River* by Bill Thompson; many websites, especially www.discoverpowellriver.com

Copyright © Tara Chernoff and Emma Levez Larocque 2005

Thanks to our sponsors: Powell River Credit Union Financial Group, Pacific Coastal Airlines, Laughing Oyster Restaurant, District of Powell River, Powell River Sea Kayak, Oceanview Helicopters, Westview Realty, NorskeCanada, Weyerhaeuser, Myrtle Point Golf Club, The Historic Lund Hotel, and Lakeside Floating Vacations.
Also, thanks to the businesses and organizations in Powell River who pre-bought books to help support this project.

Special thanks to Matt Larocque, Will, Joshua, Christopher, and Jeffrey Chernoff, Melany Hallam and Derek Johnson, Steve and Nancy Howlin, Kate Spanks and Stu Sveinson, and Mayor Stewart Alsgard, who helped make this book possible.

Cover photo: Jervis Inlet: Ferry coming in to Saltery Bay
Title Page photo: Walking on one of Powell River's many trails
Dedication Page photo: The Back Country and Mount Diadem

ISBN 0-9737937-0-8

Printed in Canada

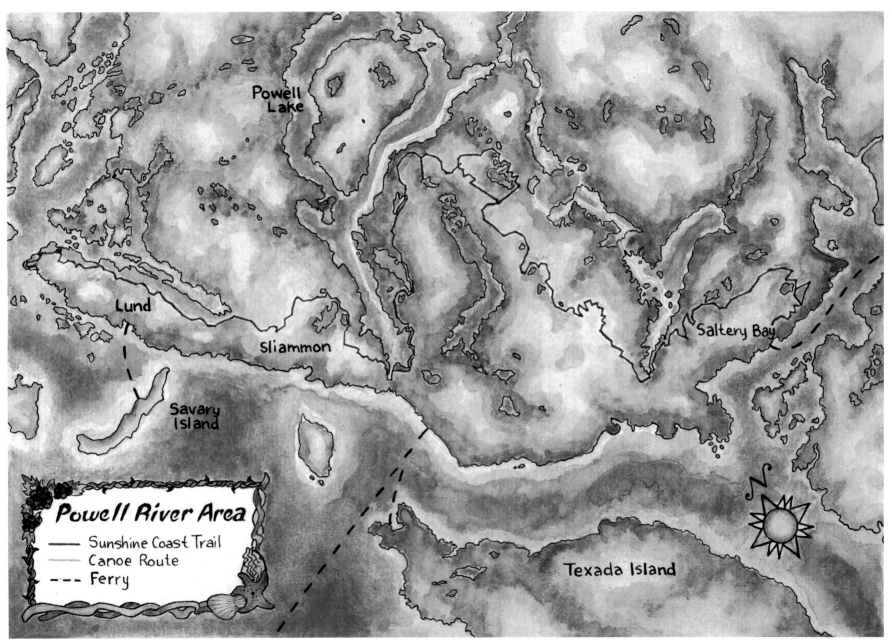

Powell Lake

Lund

Sliammon

Savary Island

Saltery Bay

Powell River Area

—— Sunshine Coast Trail
—— Canoe Route
--- Ferry

Texada Island

Artwork by Abby-Gail J. Hyldig

FORWARD

Few places in the world present such incredible beauty on both a small and large scale as does Powell River, British Columbia, now observing its fiftieth year since incorporation, the Pearl on the Sunshine Coast and a Cultural Capital of Canada!

This splendid book presents an incredible variety of visual exposures, harmonizing nature and population. It is a refreshing and imaginative departure from traditional pictorial presentations. The photographs virtually come alive. The natural fragility of our area, which we so often take for granted, demands our duty of sensitive stewardship.

The variety of images portray a great culture, heritage and tradition of the First Nation people of Tla'amin [Sliammon], whose traditional territory we recognize and respect. The citizens of Powell River are acutely aware of the combined challenges and successes in building community-to-community relations. The First Nation elders and the senior citizens of Powell River teach us respect and how to appreciate what we have. They emphasize the importance of natural beauty, what it brings to us and how the human imprint must understand and respect the delicate balance we share.

Our citizens, youth and adults, strive for success and envision balancing what we have with inevitable future growth. There is something here for everyone. Ideas abound and are discussed, debated, balanced, and implemented. Powell River (Ayjoomixw) offers a wonderful combination of cultural, educational, sports and recreational facilities, a safe community, health care, compassionate assisted living and extended care, volunteers, affordable living, nature sites, parks, lakes, the sea, walking trails, rich flora and fauna and unique history.

Prepare yourselves to enjoy a great feast for the senses as you delve into this wonderful book and share the joy of the jewel with us. Come see us and become part of the great development of a balanced economic and natural vision for the future. Remember, we are all inhabitants of biosphere earth.

Stewart B. Alsgard
Mayor

For Matt and Will, our husbands, whose support and love inspires us to make the most of life's adventures.
– Emma Levez Larocque and Tara Chernoff

BLACKBERRY
Rubus discolor

It is quite safe to say that if Powell River had an official berry, the blackberry would be it. A nuisance to some and a blessing to others, blackberry vines are ruthlessly determined and ever-present in and around Powell River. The thorny vines bloom with white flowers in early summer, and by August, succulent berries are drooping from the bushes.

Two varieties of blackberry grow in this area: the native species *Rubus ursinus*; and the more common *Rubus discolor*, or Himalayan Blackberry, which originated in Eurasia. A member of the rose family, the Himalayan Blackberry has an arched bramble with sturdy stems, and its success is due to the fact that its root system is deep and extensive. Its flowers need no pollination and a single blackberry bush can produce between seven thousand and thirteen thousand seeds. Seeds are spread by animals and gravity.

Powell Riverites have embraced the blackberry as part of their culture, and each year the town holds a popular festival at the peak of blackberry season to celebrate it. The highlight of The Blackberry Festival is the street party, at which the whole of Marine Avenue shuts down so that locals can gather to enjoy music, entertainment, and food, including (of course!) a plethora of blackberry desserts and drinks.

SEA KAYAKING
Okeover Inlet

A whole new way to explore the world. That's how first-time kayakers describe this tranquil form of water transportation. Travelling by kayak provides the opportunity to discover nooks and crannies forbidden to larger vessels. Poised just above the water's surface, a kayaker is able to take a closer look at sea life, or investigate the shallows of hidden coves and inlets. In deeper waters kayakers sometimes experience close encounters with seals, whales or dolphins.

Many fabulous destinations are accessible from different parts of the Upper Sunshine Coast, and this watery playground accommodates single and multi-day trips. Launching from Lund, it is possible to kayak to Savary Island or putter around the Copeland Islands (known to locals as The Raggeds). Okeover Inlet is a sheltered location with plenty of interesting coastline. From Powell River it is a short paddle out to the breakwater hulks at the mill, whose immensity is best felt from the seat of a kayak! St. Vincent's Bay and Hardy Island are great day-trips from Saltery Bay.

Taking the time for multi-day trips means it is possible to reach some exceptionally beautiful and pristine areas. Desolation Sound Marine Park, one of British Columbia's largest, is only a few kilometres from Lund, and several days can be happily spent exploring it. Toba and Bute Inlets are further north, nestled within the Coast Mountains. Jedediah and Lasqueti islands lie south of Texada Island, and also offer unique paddling experiences for those who want to get off the beaten path. Although it is easy to get caught up in the excitement of kayaking in this spectacular area, it is important to plan well for a trip of any length. Weather and currents are always factors in open water: local kayak companies can provide information about potential hazards, as well as tours, lessons, and rental equipment.

THE CORPORATION OF THE DISTRICT OF POWELL RIVER
Historical Townsite

Visitors are filled with a sense of the past as they wander around Powell River's Historic Townsite. Once known itself as Powell River, the creation of Townsite began around 1910.

Originally the Powell River Company – which owned and operated the local pulp and paper mill – constructed and owned all of the houses and public buildings in Townsite. The company built not only a town, but a lifestyle for its workers. The owners paid for the construction of sports facilities and encouraged leisure activities such as baseball, golf, music, drama and fine arts. Dwight Hall, pictured here, was built in 1927 as a place to hold dances and other events. It is still a much-loved venue today. Boss's Row, a line of beautiful old houses where company managers lived, and the Patricia Theatre, the oldest continuously operating movie theatre in Canada, are other features of Townsite. This fascinating part of Powell River was designated a National Historic District by the federal government in 1995.

In the early years, the areas that surrounded Townsite, like Cranberry Lake, Westview and Wildwood, had identities of their own. As the mill expanded, so did the need for further accommodation. Cranberry Lake was the first "suburb" of Powell River because it was within walking distance of the mill. Lots were allocated for homesteaders in Westview and Wildwood, some of which were taken by soldiers returning from World War I. In 1954 the Powell River Company began selling the houses it owned, and the people of Townsite started contemplating the formation of a municipality. With encouragement from the provincial government – and resistance from some local residents – in 1955 Townsite, Westview, Cranberry Lake, and Wildwood amalgamated to form the Corporation of the District of Powell River (CDPR).

Powell River's history is something to be treasured, as its present is to be celebrated, and its future anticipated. Fifty years after incorporation, the town's business centre has shifted to Westview, but work between the three levels of local government, Sliammon, CDPR and the Regional District of Powell River, continues to draw citizens of the entire Upper Sunshine Coast together.

Powell River
The Pearl on the Sunshine Coast

POWELL LAKE
North of Powell River

On sunny summer afternoons people along the Upper Sunshine Coast head out to play, and one of their favourite places to go is a lake located in Powell River's backyard. Powell Lake stretches over a distance of 51 kilometres, and it boasts 450 kilometres of picturesque shoreline. Once an inlet of the ocean, the lake is 416 metres at its deepest. It is a freshwater lake, but a layer of ancient seawater 150 metres down tells a story of the Ice Age, before glaciers receded and the lake became landlocked. Powell Lake is connected to Goat Lake by a channel. It is easily accessed at several points, including Mowat Bay, Haywire Bay, and the marina at the Shingle Mill.

The charm of Powell Lake has long been appreciated; it has been a favoured weekend and holiday destination since the early 1900s. Over the last century many families have built cabins and floating houses along the shoreline. There is currently a moratorium on further development of the area, but the lake is still a place to which people flock in the summer months. The size of Powell Lake means that those willing to travel further afield can always find a quiet corner, and there are many activities to be enjoyed. Take a swim in the cool, clear water; go for a hike in flourishing forests that line the lake; spend a morning in splendid solitude fishing for a variety of species; take a boat tour, and don't forget the waterskis! Several companies rent houseboats or cabins, so that visitors from all over the world can enjoy the luxuries of Powell Lake.

The adjacent photo shows just one portion of Powell Lake, looking up to the Eldred River, which feeds Goat Lake, with Goat Island in the foreground (on the left).

FISHING

Saltery Bay Campground

The Upper Sunshine Coast is an ideal holiday destination for people who enjoy recreational fishing. Numerous lakes and sheltered ocean waters create the perfect environment for many different kinds of angling. There are a wide variety of resident fish, and many migrant species that pass through the area.

The best time to go saltwater fishing is from late May until September, when many migratory fish make their way through Malaspina and Georgia straits. Some saltwater hotspots, as listed on the website www.proutdoors.com include: Coho (Kiddie) Point and Blubber Bay at the north end of Texada Island; Grant Reef; Lund; Albion Point; and the waters around Harwood Island. Because there are so many great fishing holes close by, the pastime can be enjoyed by anyone with a small boat and a fishing rod.

Many locals and visitors also enjoy freshwater fishing around Powell River. Cutthroat Trout is the main species in the area, but Rainbow Trout and Kokanee Salmon are also common. Most lakes on the Upper Sunshine Coast are open year-round, but Powell Lake, Goat Lake and Inland Lake are closed for fishing from November 1 until March 31. Some other recommended freshwater fishing locales include the Eldred River, and Nanton, Lois, Windsor, Tony and Lewis lakes. Knowledgeable local outdoor-store owners can provide advice on licences, methods, tackle, and fishing locations.

WILLINGDON BEACH TRAIL
Westview

Willingdon Beach is located in the heart of Powell River, and it is a favourite gathering place for locals and visitors alike. This beautiful spot contains a sandy beach, a large, grassy park, a campground, a water park, and a playground. Willingdon Beach was originally a logging dumpsite known as Michigan's Landing. It was used in this manner between 1910 and 1918. In 1928, it was officially renamed after Lord Willingdon, Governor General of Canada at the time.

At the north end of the park, the 1.2-kilometre Willingdon Beach Trail begins. This historic trail was originally a logging railway used by the Michigan-Puget Sound Logging Company. After its years as a railway ended, a local man named Bill Fishleigh lobbied the Powell River Company to remove the old logging ties so the trail could be made into a cycle path. Until the road between Westview and Townsite was built, it was the main route between the mill and Westview. For fifteen years Bill volunteered his time to maintain the path.

Today the trail is maintained by members of the Powell River Forestry Museum Society, a non-profit organization dedicated to the education, preservation and public awareness of the forest history of the Powell River area. Displays of old logging equipment – including a massive steam donkey – pepper the trail. Signs draw visitors' attention to a few remaining old-growth trees, and the wide variety of species, such as Broadleaf Maple, Red Alder, Douglas Fir, Grand Fir, and Western Red Cedar. The Willingdon Beach Trail is one of the most popular walking trails in Powell River, and is used annually for the Bruce Denniston Spirit Run as well as a variety of other events.

TEXADA ISLAND
Marble Bay

Intriguing is a word that describes Texada Island perfectly. From its spirited history to its unique flower rock (pictured below) and its famous sandcastle competition, this Spanish-named island is a memorable place to visit. At 51 kilometres long and almost 10 kilometres at its widest, Texada is the largest of the Gulf Islands. It was named by Don Jose Navarez, a Spanish seaman, around 1791.

Many locations on the island are identified by activities that occurred there in the days of the first settlers. Blubber Bay, for example, was named because of a whale processing station that once existed there (though no one is sure of its size). In 1871 iron ore was discovered on the northwest coast, and a few years later marble was found on the island. Marble Bay (pictured on the adjacent page) is the place where marble was first taken from Texada. Then gold and copper were found. The Gold Rush was on, and news of the discovery brought many men seeking their fortune to the island. Between mining and logging, Texada became a busy place. The population grew quickly, as did the town. There were three hotels with saloons, a hospital, several stores and businesses, and rumour has it there was even an opera house. There was also a distillery in Pocahontas Bay, which supplied liquor to the United States during Prohibition.

A series of three fires, which destroyed most of the buildings on Texada, occurred in the 1910s, and the promise of riches through gold didn't last. But some of the people who had come settled anyway, and the community thrived. The mining focus turned to limestone quarrying, which helped Texadans survive through the difficult 1930s. Limestone and aggregates remain a major industry on the island to the present day.

Approximately twelve hundred people, mostly divided between the communities of Van Anda and Gillies Bay, currently live on Texada Island. It is a beautiful, friendly place with much to offer in the way of outdoor activities like hiking, biking and camping. Texada lies about eight kilometres southwest of Powell River and can be accessed by ferry.

Photo by Lorrie Pirart

TOTEM POLE
Viewpoint, Westview

On June 21, 2004, two colourful totem poles were erected at the Viewpoint in Westview. They have quickly become well-known images in Powell River, and the piece on the left demands particular attention. Looking closely, one is reminded that every detail holds significance. It is the creation of Master Carver Jackie Timothy, a renowned Coast Salish artist.

"I wanted to show the communities of Powell River and Sliammon joining together," Jackie says. "It was also important to include the heritage and culture of the Sliammon First Nations people. And somehow I wanted to represent the past, present, and future."

Creative inspiration for the totem pole came to him in a dream of his people before any influence from the outside world, and a potlatch celebration. He saw a grandfather and grandson travelling after the potlatch; they stopped to start a fire. The boy asked his grandfather if their people would still be singing, dancing and drumming in the future, and his grandfather replied that maybe someone would have a vision, and they would know. The grandfather walked away for a few minutes, and the boy watched as a circle cleared in the smoke above the fire. He could see something inside the circle, so he peered closer. What he saw was a scene from the future: June 21, 2004. He saw his people still singing, still dancing, still drumming. But there was something different. There were people with light skin – people like he had never seen before. Still, they were all happy and laughing. From this dream Jackie formed the image of a boy peering into a circle, which is portrayed in several of the eyes on the totem pole.

The 6-metre creation honours the hereditary chiefs of the Sliammon people. The animals depicted on the pole – the eagle, bear, and frog – are representative of creatures that have been associated with the Coast Salish people for centuries. The face on the chest of the eagle represents the spirit of life, and the double-headed snake symbolizes the coming together of the Powell River and Sliammon communities. Several other totem poles have been erected around Powell River. Each tells a story, and brings a new awareness of Sliammon culture to the people who live in and visit Powell River.

PACIFIC WHITE-SIDED DOLPHIN
Lagenorhynchus obliquidens

The Pacific White-Sided Dolphin is dark grey or black in colour with a white or light grey stripe along the flank. Its belly is white, but its beak, flippers, flukes, and the front of its dorsal fin are dark. This species inhabits the entire Pacific range, and though it is considered a deep-water species, it has been spotted closer to shore and in inland waters in recent years. The Pacific White-Sided Dolphin usually travels in large groups, and it loves to play – bow riding, surfing, leaping and somersaulting. Magic moments can happen when someone is lucky enough to be in the right place at the right time.

Texada Island photographer Lorrie Pirart was out fishing in his 16-foot aluminum boat one day when he experienced such a moment. It all began when he looked up and saw a black line coming toward him.

"I didn't know what it was for sure, so I shut my engine off and waited, and it turned out it was dolphins. There must have been about fifty of them and they came right to me." Lorrie took out his camera. "They were all around me – at the bow, at the stern, right underneath me!" In total he spent an hour-and-a-half watching and photographing the dolphins, moving his boat slowly back into their path as they travelled, waiting for them to come to him. They turned into Gillies Bay, on the west side of Texada Island, and swam along the shore. Then the show began. "They were jumping right beside my boat. Some of them were leaping as high as three times their body length." This picture is from that incredible day. It was taken as the dolphins were coming out of Gillies Bay and heading towards Comox.

Photo by Lorrie Pirart

23

NUN KUM DANCERS
Sliammon First Nation

As people learn and experience the songs and dances of the Sliammon First Nation, the songs gain power. That is one thing that has inspired Erik Blaney, leader of the Nun Kum Dancers, to collect, learn, teach and perform the music and movements of his people. He started the Nun Kum Dancers when he was just nine years old. He says his mother was the driving force. "She handed me a drum and said, 'Drum, and I'll sing.'"

Erik, whose childhood name was Menathey, or Drummer Boy, has often drawn inspiration from his great, great grandfather, Pehlex, who was the last known shaman healer of the Sliammon people. "That is why I felt it was in me to help heal through drumming and singing. Because of him I knew what needed to be done." Erik has continued his grandfather's legacy by helping to bring traditional songs and dances to the young people of Sliammon. He has spent a great deal of energy finding lost songs, and is passionate about sharing them with others, and making sure that they are not forgotten again. He, and the rest of the Nun Kum Dancers, want people from different cultures to experience their music. "We want to let everyone hear the songs, and then they will dig more into the history of what happened [to our people], and learn about how we can all come together now. The songs belong to everyone."

More than twenty young people between the ages of three and twenty-two are now part of the dance group. They practice once a week and perform several times a month during the summer. They have performed at large venues like the Pan Asia International Exhibition and Kathaumixw, as well as smaller events like elders' gatherings, Sea Fair and Blackberry Festival. In the adjacent photograph, Erik is pictured performing *The Eagle* with the Nun Kum Dancers at Kathaumixw 2004.

Photo courtesy of the Powell River Academy of Music

SAILING
Willingdon Beach

Weather, sunshine, wind, and saltwater on your face. Sailing is a popular pastime on the Upper Sunshine Coast. On any given good-weather day, passersby can look out on Malaspina Strait to see sailboats on the horizon. Many of the sailors in Powell River and area belong to the Powell River Sailing Club.

The club was started in 1967 by a handful of families who were interested in sharing their love for the sport. Les Moss was one of the charter members of the group. He started sailing in 1964, when there were only three or four sailboats in the harbour at Powell River. "Sailing is all about learning how to survive on the water," he says. "It's about the challenge of making your boat go exactly where you want it to – and making it go just a little bit faster than the one beside you...It's about the feeling of awe you get about the world when you are out on the water."

Today more than thirty families belong to the sailing club. The club holds weekly events and races between April and October, as well as scattered events throughout the winter months. New members are welcome – there is always a boat that needs extra crewmembers. Above all, the club is about the camaraderie of being with other people and sharing a passion for sailing.

POWELL RIVER CREDIT UNION FINANCIAL GROUP
Since 1939

Businesses that find their way into the heart of a town say a lot about the people who live there. The Credit Union has been an important part of the Powell River community since the town was granted the first Credit Union charter in British Columbia in 1939. The Powell River Credit Union is a community-owned financial institution where people invest in one another and share the benefits. As a locally owned and operated company, all decisions are made right in Powell River. Profits from the company are returned to members in the form of dividends, or re-invested in the community by way of donations and sponsorships on behalf of the members.

The Powell River Credit Union had humble beginnings. It started with only thirty members, and made a profit of $0.39 in its first year of operation. But the concept was good, and it caught on. More than sixty-five years later, the company has accumulated over $112 million in assets, and its membership exceeds seven thousand people. The founders and leaders who have directed the Credit Union over the years have constantly looked to the future, and they have not been afraid of change. Today the Powell River Credit Union Financial Group operates as a modern financial institution offering all the traditional banking services, and insurance, investments, and travel services as well.

One of the reasons the company has been so successful is because of its resolution to make community involvement a priority. Over the years it has offered several programs and services that are still remembered fondly today. The Powell River Credit Union Financial Group has been recognized time and again for outstanding community involvement and the work it has done with youth. Recently, it launched a new program for high school students called CU FLY. In 2004, the Financial Group was named Business of the Year at the Chamber of Commerce Business Horizon Awards. But the people behind the scenes take it in stride. Afterall, that's what it's all about: People before profits.

GOLFING
Myrtle Point

"One bright spring afternoon 26 years ago, a strange – and almost fearful spectacle was seen on the old Powell River football ground. A one-man show was in progress. A man clad in plus-fours, with an iron club in his hand, was driving a little white ball across the rough pasture that had been hewed out for a football field. The ball driver was the late Dr. Andrew Henderson, chief medical officer at Powell River. In this incident is found the origin of golf in our town." (*Powell River Digester*, March-April 1948.)

Dr. Henderson and his golfing partner, Mrs. Janet McIntyre, are credited with introducing the sport to Powell River. It didn't take long to catch on. In the 1920s the Powell River Golf Club was formed, and the game gained popularity in leaps and bounds. The Powell River Company encouraged its employees to play the sport, and distributed one golf club to each member. Consequently, many early golfers learned to play all their shots with one type of club. Some of them remember that numerous hours were spent searching for the 15-cent rubber golf balls that were used in the game at the time.

Today the Upper Sunshine Coast boasts several beautiful golf courses including one eighteen-hole course. Enthusiasts of the game are no longer required to practice wherever they can find a flat spot; modern facilities accommodate all levels of playing ability, from novice to expert. Annual tournaments and regular events bring golfers to Powell River from near and far.

Golfing offers the opportunity to relax with friends, take a breath of fresh air, and exercise mind and body all at once. Striking scenery, including snow-capped mountains and the occasional glimpse of the ocean, lends itself to a gratifying golfing experience. Sporadic sightings of elk, deer, eagles, and other birds enhance the atmosphere. Thanks to the mild climate, the Upper Sunshine Coast is the perfect place for avid golfers at any time of year.

SAVARY ISLAND
Georgia Strait

A little taste of paradise. Savary Island, with its white, sand beaches, warm waters and abundant seafood, is as alluring as its name. This lovely island has attracted visitors since the early 1900s, and was at one time a summer meeting place for the Sliammon First Nation. Captain George Vancouver named the island "Savary's Isle" when he passed through the area in 1792. It was known as "Ayhus" to the Sliammon people. Their legend says the island was formed from a mischievous double-headed serpent. The Great Transformer turned the serpent into an island after it went on a binge, greedily devouring seals, salmon, whales, men, women and children.

Roughly 8 kilometres long and 1 kilometre wide, Savary has been nicknamed the Hawaii of the North. Its shores, with the exception of Mace Point (Green Point) at the eastern tip of the island, are white and sandy. The waters around Savary are relatively warm because of the situation of the island, and the fact that there is a sun-baked shelf on the south side. No bears, cougars, raccoons or rats live there, but deer are common. Mink and otter make sporadic visits along with bald eagles, hummingbirds and a variety of migratory bird species.

Taking a trip to Savary is like venturing into another world. Transportation to the island is by boat or water taxi. Vehicles must be barged to the island and there are no paved roads once they get there. Until the 1990s there were very few cars on Savary; even today most people travel by bicycle, or on foot. Hiking and biking trails wind through the forests, making it easy to get around. Although there are several types of accommodation on the island, visitors should be aware that there is limited camping on Savary, and no public toilets. Some basic amenities are available, but it is necessary to acquire most supplies from the mainland.

FRUIT TREES
From Saltery Bay to Lund

When fruit trees begin to blossom in the spring, pink and white blooms line the streets, filling the air with a delicious fragrance. As the winds of the season blow, their fragile petals scatter. It is a marvelous time of year.

Despite the fact that few fruit tree species are native to this area, an impressive variety of apple, cherry, plum and pear trees flourish between Saltery Bay and Lund. Small orchards have long thrived in places like Wildwood and Olsen Valley. Many of these trees originated when new people settled in the area. Eager to start their own gardens, they brought cuttings (scions) with them and grafted the scions to purchased rootstock, creating new trees.

Some of the most common apple trees along this part of the coast can be traced to an apple salesman called Mr. Brown, who is rumoured to have travelled in the area in the early part of the 20th Century. Golden Delicious, Gravenstein, Winter Banana, Duchess of Oldenburg, King, and Snow apple trees are all common to the Upper Sunshine Coast. Today, about twenty people in Powell River continue the tradition of protecting old fruit tree varieties. As members of the BC Fruit Testers Association, their role is not only to test and evaluate new species, but also to provide information and preserve old varieties of fruit bearing trees, shrubs and plants.

Throughout the summer, abundance brings a feeling of extraordinary natural wealth and good fortune. It is a time of sharing and generosity. Friends and neighbours give away cherries, plums and apples by the bucketful. Pies and preserves exchange hands. From the beginning of fruit season to the end, locals are blessed with an amazing variety of visual and appetizing treats to savour.

POWERBOATING
Malaspina Strait

Untie from the dock, toss the lines, and go. The sense of freedom that accompanies powerboating in the Upper Sunshine Coast area attracts many enthusiasts to this exciting and invigorating hobby. A world of marine destinations awaits the skipper and crew heading into the waters around Powell River.

An hour's run southeast brings boaters in range of lively Pender Harbour, serene Thormanby Island or historic Jedediah Provincial Marine Park. Accessible by Jervis Inlet are Princess Louisa Provincial Marine Park and the spectacular Chatterbox Falls. Directly across the Malaspina Strait, boaters from Powell River can take in the Comox waterfront with its medley of pubs and restaurants, or go for a stroll on Denman Island or Hornby Island. Within thirty minutes north of Powell River, powerboaters can reach sandy Savary Island or the village of Lund. A little further along lies Cortes Island and its charming coastal communities. Nearby is Desolation Sound, enclosing scads of sheltered anchorages.

Because there are so many dazzling choices, Powell River is home to a substantial number of boating enthusiasts, and the area sees many visiting boaters each year. One of the best ways to learn about all the "secret" spots is to hook up with a veteran boater. However, the excitement of making your own discoveries is equally appealing. And you can't go wrong: there are hikes and stops of interest around every corner. Rafting up with friends is an enjoyable way to spend the evening.

With dozens of freshwater lakes in the area, there are also abundant choices for boaters who prefer less salty climes. Powell Lake and Goat Lake are two well-liked freshwater destinations.

INLAND LAKE
Powell River

Just 12 kilometres by road north of the hustle bustle of Powell River is an oasis for nature lovers. Inland Lake (also known as Loon Lake) is a popular weekend destination for locals and visitors alike. The lake itself is 5.5 kilometres long, and it is encircled by a 13-kilometre wheelchair accessible trail that takes visitors past a variety of wildlife habitats, artistic carvings, campsites and picnic areas. Hiking, biking, swimming, canoeing and fishing are all activities frequently enjoyed there.

In 1956 the south end of the lake was designated a park reserve, but construction of the Inland Lake Trail System didn't begin until 1983. The idea to build a trail available to all people was inspired by Rick Hansen's Man in Motion World Tour. It was built by members of the Sunshine Coast Forest District over a period of six years, and by the time it was finished, the goal to make it completely wheelchair accessible had been achieved. In 1989 it received the Premier's Award for Excellence in Accessible Design. For more than a decade Inland Lake has been the site of the annual Loon Lake Race, which raises money for the Special Olympics. It usually attracts between sixty and one hundred participants.

Wildlife is abundant in this peaceful place. Many birds, like loons, eagles, grouse, trumpeter swans and ducks make this haven their home. Beavers, otters, cougars, deer and bears all live in the area, although they avoid humans and sightings are unusual. Small animals like chipmunks, garter snakes, frogs, and toads are more commonly seen.

MOUNTAIN BIKING
Hamill (West) Lake

Leaping over roots, balancing precariously along fallen logs, zipping up hills and down through chutes, mountain biking in Powell River is a challenging and fun-filled pastime. There are a vast number of accessible trails for adventure-seeking bikers to choose from, and their levels of difficulty vary. The scenery along the way (if you have time to pay attention!) is spectacular. Trails lead to gushing waterfalls, serene lakesides and other beautiful views. Because the climate around Powell River is one of the mildest in Canada, biking season never ends.

The close proximity of trails to town means that riders can be speeding through forests within minutes of setting out from home. Some of the best-loved trails are Myrtle Springs, the Ground Pound, Hamill (West) Lake, Suicide Creek, Bogey's Trail, the Mexican Jumping Bean, and Mud Lake. There is also great mountain biking on Texada Island. Although there are no organized biking clubs, there are many avid bikers who meet weekly to ride together. Local bike shops are a good place to get information about trails and organized rides. Maps are also available at the Visitor's Information Centre on Marine Avenue.

There are several destinations for those looking for a slower pace, or family-oriented rides. The Inland Lake Trail and the Willingdon Beach Trail are two of the most popular; the Blue Trail Loop offers a slightly more demanding ride. As well as sport and recreation, cycling is a popular form of transportation. From Powell River to Saltery Bay, Highway 101 offers wide shoulders on either side of the road to accommodate cyclists. Many tourists enjoy road biking in this area. The Circle Tour, which includes Vancouver Island, the Upper Sunshine Coast, Lower Sunshine Coast and Vancouver, is a frequently travelled route.

LAUGHING OYSTER RESTAURANT
Okeover

Ready your senses. Prepare for a tantalizing treat. The Laughing Oyster is one of Powell River's best-loved restaurants – and it's about so much more than the delectable food. It's a dining experience that will surpass the highest expectations. From the amazing oceanfront setting to the excellent service and gourmet food, there isn't a detail that goes unnoticed.

Everything at the Laughing Oyster is delightfully fresh. Flowers cut from the garden adorn every table. Spices, many ingredients of which come from the restaurant's herb garden, are made on site. Fresh (often local) fare is available daily. Although the restaurant is famous for its seafood – in particular its signature dish, Seafood Harvest for Two – it caters to all appetites with an extensive mouth-watering menu. When in season, various fruits from trees surrounding the restaurant are used in scrumptious desserts.

The trees that bear these gifts hint of the past, before the Laughing Oyster Restaurant existed. At one time the property belonged to homesteaders John Oscar and Nanni Roos. In 1908 John Oscar Roos, a Swede who worked his way across Canada on the railroad, arrived in Lund. He started working at the Lund Hotel as a bartender, and that's where he met Nanni, a Finnish chambermaid. Despite the fact that they spoke different languages, they married and bought 65 hectares of land to homestead. They had five children. A few of their descendents, including grandson Sheldon Ahola, still live in the area.

"The Laughing Oyster Restaurant now sits where the original house was," Sheldon says. "It burned down after my grandfather died [around 1961], and my grandmother had it rebuilt." The house was converted into a restaurant, and the property changed hands a couple of times before the current owners bought it in 1998.

Today, many people are able to enjoy this incredible spot. The Laughing Oyster is accessible by water or road. It is a favourite stop for boaters heading to Desolation Sound.

Laughing Oyster
RESTAURANT

THE HULKS
Powell River Townsite

As the largest floating breakwater in the world, the hulks bring a certain amount of history and intrigue to the waters around Powell River. For many years these steel, wood and concrete ships have provided shelter for Powell River's millpond. Altogether, nineteen ships have been used in the breakwater since 1930. They came from all over the world, boasting pasts full of adventure, as documented in *Hulks: The Breakwater Ships of Powell River* by local author John A. Campbell. In their heydays, they played a variety of roles; among them, battleships, log barges, merchant vessels, and oil tankers.

One of British Columbia's most famous ships, the *Malahat*, has a connection to the breakwater hulks. During US Prohibition in the 1920s, the *Malahat* was used as the mother ship to the rum fleet. Known as the Queen of Rum Row, it carried and distributed cases of liquor to speedboats just outside US territorial waters. In 1945, close to the end of its colourful life, the *Malahat*'s hulk was purchased by the Powell River mill for use in the breakwater. Because of its poor condition upon arrival, it was never used for that purpose. It succumbed to a great coastal storm, and now lies just outside the log pond by the rock breakwater. Today the wreck of the *Malahat* is a popular destination for scuba divers.

Many tales have been told about the breakwater hulks over the years. Today ten concrete hulks can still be seen from the Viewpoint in Townsite. Their presence is frequently marked by the barking of sea lions seeking shelter from rough seas.

GREAT BLUE HERON
Ardea herodias

A person doesn't have to go far to find wildlife on the Upper Sunshine Coast. Sighting animals and birds within the boundaries of town is one of the very special things about Powell River, Lund and other settlements in the area. Driving along Marine Avenue – part of Highway 101 – it is difficult not to notice the numerous herons that nest in the trees and meander along the shore there. Glancing down from the highway towards the ocean at low tide, it is common to see several of these long-legged creatures fishing for a meal or wading among the rocks.

With its stick-like legs and long, elegant neck, the Great Blue Heron is the largest heron in North America. Its back and wings are blue-grey, its belly is whitish with black streaking, and it has a striking black stripe on its head that ends in a plume behind the eye. It uses its long, sharp bill to catch fish and other prey. This bird spends most of its day foraging for food, but the majority of its activity takes place around dawn and dusk. It eats a combination of fish, frogs, salamanders, lizards, snakes, shrimps, crabs, crayfish, dragonflies, grasshoppers, and aquatic insects.

The Great Blue Heron is a shy creature, and it is fairly quiet, unless startled or threatened. Because many eagles also nest in the trees along Marine Avenue, it is not unusual for passersby to witness a noisy argument between an eagle – who is skulking around a heron nest looking for a snack – and a group of herons.

SEAWALK
Westview

Strolling along the edge of the ocean is a wonderful way to spend an evening, and Powell River's Seawalk allows people to do just that. The 1.3-kilometre walkway that winds along the shore was the initiative of the District of Powell River. It was funded by the municipality and the Ministry of Transportation. Not only does the walkway provide increased stability to Highway 101, it also offers locals and visitors a beautiful place to mosey.

When the Seawalk was constructed, a cultural component was included. Several benches with colourful First Nations carvings are featured on the path. They, along with two totem poles that were erected at the Viewpoint above the Seawalk, enhance the beauty and interest of the walkway. Other benches have also been placed along the length of the Seawalk so people can stop, rest and appreciate the view.

On sunny days walkers make their way down to this special path to enjoy the sights, smells and sounds of nature. Brightly coloured flowers and greenery that line the banks make the setting beautifully natural, and their fragrances mix with the salty smell of the ocean. Birds chirp to background music of waves lapping against the shore. The Seawalk is a great spot to watch the sun as it settles on the horizon. It is a place to experience the best of nature, right on the edge of town.

The Seawalk can be accessed from several points: the Viewpoint in Westview; the barge terminal at the north end; and a couple of pathways at the south end.

LUND HARBOUR

The Gateway to Desolation Sound

Because of its strategic location, Lund Harbour has been used for many years as an access point to the Lund area (called Gl'amin by the Coast Salish people). Gl'amin was first settled by the Sliammon, Klahoose and Homalco peoples. Because of the way it is positioned, the harbour allowed early detection of travellers, which was useful for defense purposes.

In 1889 Swedes Fred and Charlie Thulin came to the then-deserted Gl'amin and renamed it Lund after the Swedish city. Their goal was to develop Lund into a successful coastal waypoint. They logged in the area and built the first wharf, which quickly developed into a busy spot with logging company tugboats dropping off mail and supplies for forestry workers in the vicinity. By 1892 Lund had one of only two certified post offices operating north of Vancouver. The town continued to grow and the harbour grew with it.

Today Lund Harbour is well known to local and visiting boaters. It is located at the gateway to spectacular Desolation Sound, and many boaters venturing further up the coast stop there to stock up on supplies. Many services are offered within walking distance, including a bakery, a grocery and liquor store, restaurants, a hotel, and kayak and diving rentals. The harbour is also home to a fleet of prawn boats, sailboats and recreational boats.

WINTER SPORTS
The Knuckleheads

You can play in the sand in the morning, and the snow in the afternoon. That is one of the great things about the Upper Sunshine Coast area. Winter sports are not as prevalent in Powell River as they are in colder parts of Canada, but for those dedicated to seeking out the white stuff, there are several options. One of the most popular places to go snowshoeing, skiing and snowmobiling around Powell River is the gentle sloping hills of the Knuckleheads, part of the Coast Mountain range. The highest peak in the Knuckleheads, which were named for their shape, has an elevation of more than 1600 metres. There is an unofficial recreation area of about 3 by 5 kilometres, which is part of the Powell Provincial Forest.

Members of the Mount Diadem Ski Club first "discovered" the Knuckleheads recreation area. They started skiing there around 1959 and continued until 1977 when their main ski lodge burned down. Twenty years later people started thinking about developing the area for use again. In 1998 a new organization – The Knuckleheads Winter Recreation Association – fixed up one of the old rope tow sheds and made it into a comfortable cabin that can accommodate eight people overnight. They also cleared overgrown trails and opened the area, accessed off the old logging road called E-Branch, up to the public again. In 2002 the association, with the help of the Rotary Club and donations from several local businesses, built a second cabin reached by the nearby A-Branch.

Although there are presently no organized clubs, hundreds of people go up to the Knuckleheads every year, their presence recorded in cabin logbooks. Snowshoeing, cross-country skiing, snowboarding and snowmobiling can all be enjoyed in the area between November and May. Granite Lake, the Bunster Hills and Elephant Lakes are other favoured locations for winter sports on the Upper Sunshine Coast.

MUSIC
International Choral Kathaumixw and more

Sounds of music speed through the air; melodies escape under doors and are carried on the wind. They are heard far and wide. Music has been a keystone in Powell River since its' early days, and in recent years it has brought the town a certain amount of fame. As early as the 1920s various musical societies were forming in Powell River, and enthusiasm for the making and appreciation of music has only strengthened over the years. Community bands and choirs have been a constant, and in 1980 the Powell River Academy of Music was founded, bringing a sense of formality to music in Powell River. Outside of the academy, many local talents also continue to thrive, both in Powell River and other communities on the Upper Sunshine Coast.

The Academy of Music has helped promote Powell River around the world as its choir members perform regularly at international festivals. It offers music lessons from esteemed teachers, provides support for local people who wish to make music their career, and brings professional musicians into the community for all to enjoy. It has also acted as the founding institution of International Choral Kathaumixw and SOAP (the Symphony Orchestra Academy of the Pacific).

Kathaumixw, which takes place over a week every second summer, is a world-renowned international choral festival. At each event about thirty-five choirs from a variety of countries come to perform and compete in Powell River. This photograph shows the Guangzhou Children's Palace Choir from China, which performed at Kathaumixw 2004. While the festival is happening, it transforms the town from a quiet, peaceful haven into an exciting stage bursting with song. Locals welcome choir members into their homes, and music is everywhere; besides the formal concerts held during the week, there are impromptu concerts on the beach, in the mall, and on the street. Through the eyes and voices of visitors, locals are reminded of the special treasure that is their home.

Photo courtesy of the Powell River Academy of Music

57

In Powell River since 1987

The remote nature of the Powell River area is part of its charm, but that is true only because it is accessible. One of the most expedient and convenient ways to access the Upper Sunshine Coast is with Pacific Coastal Airlines. Owner Daryl Smith started in the industry in 1964. Over the years he bought and sold many aircraft and airlines around British Columbia. But he always came back to the place he calls home. In 1975 he formed Powell Air in partnership with Percy Logging, and in 1980 that company took over the licence for air service between Vancouver and Powell River. Despite troubled times and changing ownership of the licence for the Powell River route, Daryl stayed involved in air service to Powell River. In 1987 he set up Pacific Coastal Airlines with a partner and has been serving Powell River under that name ever since.

"Pacific Coastal is a company that provides service to places no other airlines want to go," Daryl says with a chuckle. Logos on the tails of the airplanes hint of something special: a love and respect for the small towns and remote communities on the BC Coast and interior. A lighthouse was the first tail logo – chosen as a tribute because lighthouses along the coast were being shut down at the time. A tugboat, seine boat, elk, totem pole, grizzly bear, logging truck, sailboat, and sports fisherman are among the other tail logos that make Pacific Coastal's planes unique.

Today, Pacific Coastal Airlines is a well-established name on the Canadian West Coast. It is truly a family business with four of Daryl's sons actively involved in the management of the company. It employs more than two hundred and fifty people, operates twelve bases and flies a total of twenty aircraft. Besides servicing Powell River, Pacific Coastal provides daily flights between Vancouver and Cranbrook, Williams Lake, Anahim Lake, Victoria, Comox, Campbell River, Port Hardy, Bella Coola, Bella Bella, Masset and Klemtu. But no matter how big the company gets, Daryl never forgets where his roots are. Pacific Coastal is an important sponsor of many Powell River events, like International Choral Kathaumixw, Logger Sports and various community improvement projects.

Photograph by Emma Levez Larocque; Artwork by Abby-Gail J. Hyldig

PELAGIC CORMORANT
Phalacrocorax pelagicus

The hulks at Powell River's millpond have provided shelter for a number of sea animals and birds over the years, not the least of which is the pelagic cormorant. This interesting bird, which draws the attention of onlookers as it flaps frantically just along the waters' surface, is a capable fisher. It feeds primarily on crustaceans and other fish, sometimes diving to more than 55 metres to find food. It is said to be the deepest diver among all cormorants.

Pelagic cormorants live along coastal waters and bays, nesting in colonies on steep sea cliffs and rocky islets – and, if the opportunity occurs, on hulks. They can frequently be seen perched upright with their wings spread out for drying, and they often nest on ledges so narrow that they are forced to take off backwards, facing the cliff. Sensitive to human disturbance and environmental threats, the population of these birds is in decline.

They are the smallest of the Pacific Coast cormorants (64 to 76 centimetres) with a slim, hooked bill and a slender neck and head. Normally black in colour, they display red facial skin and bright white flank patches during breeding season. Male and female birds are similar in appearance. Sometimes pelagic cormorants use the same nest over a period of several years. By piling up seaweed, grass and ocean debris, they can create a nest that is 1.5 to 2 metres high.

Mitlenatch Island Nature Provincial Park, located in the Strait of Georgia (between Vancouver Island and the Upper Sunshine Coast), is an important nesting area for pelagic cormorants, and a number of other seabirds.

DESOLATION SOUND MARINE PARK
Prideaux Haven

One of the Upper Sunshine Coast's most famous jewels is the varied and magnificent Desolation Sound Marine Park. The sound was named by Captain George Vancouver who sailed through the area in 1792. He perceived the land and seascape to be remote and forbidding, and named it accordingly. But this dramatic locale is far from desolate. Each year its stunning scenery and sheltered anchorages draw kayakers, yachters, sailors and powerboaters from all over the world. Desolation Sound is nature at its best – sparkling waters teeming with marine life, shores lined with lush forests, frequent sightings of black bears and playful harbour seals, irresistible lakes and waterfalls – all nestled into the stunning backdrop of the snow-peaked Coast Mountains.

The park, one of the biggest in British Columbia, was created in 1973. It is made up of 5666 hectares of upland and 2570 hectares of foreshore and water, and is located at the place where Malaspina Inlet and Homfray Channel meet. The park encompasses small bays, snug coves, numerous islands and more than 60 kilometres of shoreline. In summer, its waters can warm to near-tropical temperatures, enticing even the most reluctant swimmer. For those interested in anchoring and exploring ashore, the sound offers a bounty of hiking trails, many of which lead to freshwater swimming holes.

Prideaux Haven, Tenedos Bay and Grace Harbour are three anchorages where boaters gather, but there are many isolated bays and campsites throughout, and around, the park. Desolation Sound is a wilderness area, and visitors should be prepared and self-sufficient. For more information about visiting Desolation Sound Marine Park, consult the *BC Marine Parks Guide.*

SUNSHINE COAST TRAIL

Saltery Bay to Sarah Point (Desolation Sound)

From temperate rainforests to oceanside bluffs; from alpine ridges to pristine lakes. The Sunshine Coast Trail stretches 180 kilometres from one end of the Upper Sunshine Coast to the other, connecting patches of old growth forest all along the way. The ambitious trail encompasses a wide variety of landscapes, showing off the natural beauty of the area.

Construction of the Sunshine Coast Trail began in 1992 by a group of local outdoor enthusiasts who wanted to preserve remaining ancient forests, and make them more accessible to the public. They formed a non-profit society called PRPAWS (the Powell River Parks and Wilderness Society) and began their work. One trail at a time, and with an uncountable number of volunteer hours, the trail began to take shape. More than a decade later, the Sunshine Coast Trail consists of five sections, ranging in difficulty from moderate to challenging. Significant elevation gains and losses afford spectacular extremes – panoramic views from mountaintops, swimming in the clear waters of isolated lakes or ocean beaches, and the cool relief of a mossy valley.

Because the trail is accessible from more than twenty points, it can be hiked as a series of day trips. The adjacent photograph of Eagle Walz (right), who has spearheaded the building of the Sunshine Coast Trail, and Richie Tait, a PRPAWS and BOMB (Bloody Old Men's Brigade) Squad member, was taken on a day-hike on Sliammon Lakes Trail, overlooking Thethyeth Lake. The Sunshine Coast Trail also has campsites and facilities in various stages of development all along the way, so that hikers wanting to experience the trail in a through-hike can do so.

The Sunshine Coast Trail is gaining recognition as a demanding but magnificent adventure. In July 2004 four ultra-marathoners made the first ever attempt to run the entire trail without stopping. Up-to-date information about the trail, as well as conditions and events happening on it can be found on the comprehensive website www.sunshinecoast-trail.com.

TUGBOATING
Malaspina Strait

When people look out at Malaspina Strait, they are often greeted by a familiar sight. What they see is a boat – a small, determined-looking vessel – muscling its way down the shoreline, towing behind it a barge, or a log boom. The boat is no ordinary craft, but a tugboat, slowly and steadily transporting cargo to a wide variety of destinations.

Tugboating has a long history in the Powell River area. Because of the rugged terrain along the coast, transportation by water has always been the most efficient way to move freight. For close to one hundred years, tugboats and barges have been used to convey a wide array of products: everything from food supplies and livestock to building materials and machinery. The tugboat industry has also been extremely important for the transportation of supplies and products – like logs, wood chips, chemicals and paper – to and from the Powell River mill. Kingcome Navigation, a name that has been synonymous with towing and barging for almost a century, was formed in 1910 as the log transportation arm of the Powell River Company.

A 1954 tugboating tragedy is the cause of sadness associated with the industry in Powell River. The tug *Teeshoe* sank in tragic circumstances in a December storm that year, killing three people. A twelve-year-old boy survived. The *Teeshoe* tragedy, and what has happened to the people who were affected by it, is documented in *TEESHOE: A Powell River Story* by local filmmaker Jan Padgett, released in February 2005.

OCHRE SEA STAR
Pisaster ochraceous

Wandering at low tide along ocean shores with the sun on your back and the wind ruffling your hair is a pleasure that many residents and visitors to the Upper Sunshine Coast enjoy. There is something to see in every crack and crevice: hermit crabs, tidal pools teeming with life, varieties of seaweed, beach glass, and of course the well-loved sea star.

The most common intertidal sea star in this area is the ochre sea star. Their average size is about 25 centimetres across, and they come in a variety of colours: purple, reddish, brown, yellow, and orange. Most ochre stars have five tapering arms, which are speckled with rough, white spines that form netlike or line patterns. These bumps are actually pinchers that protect them from other animals. Ochre stars have light-sensitive pigment spots at the end of their arms that help them to find safe places. The underside of their arms are covered with numerous tube feet with which they can move in any direction (the ochre star has no head, tail, or brain). They also use their feet to pry open hard mollusks like mussels, which are a main part of their diet.

Ochre stars can be found on rocky shores from Alaska to Baja California, usually well above the low-tide line. They need seawater to survive, but they can live for up to fifty hours out of the water if they are in the shade or among moist algae. Their predators include birds, large snails, and sea otters.

Sea stars are special because no matter how many times you happen across one, it's like finding a piece of treasure. Stretched out or sheltering under rocks, hiding from the sun, they are like messengers that hint of secrets from the sea.

BEACHES
Donkersley Beach

The tide comes in, the tide goes out. As the water ebbs and flows, it constantly changes the landscape of the Upper Sunshine Coast. At high tide rocky shores have a rugged beauty all their own. But as low tide approaches, sandy beaches show themselves, delighting sun seekers looking for a soft place to wriggle their toes.

There are many beach hangouts in and around Powell River, which means that most of them are never very busy. Popular oceanside locations include Donkersley and Palm beaches south of Powell River, Willingdon right in town, and Gibsons to the north. Shelter Point is a popular beach on Texada Island, and most of Savary Island's shores are renowned for their white sand, even at high tide. For those who prefer warmer, fresh water, there are also plenty of lakes with great beaches in the area.

Head towards the water for some sandcastle fun, find a quiet spot in the sand and dive into a good book, or take a refreshing dip after a long day in the hot sun. Beaches are a favourite place for locals and visitors, and not just in the summer months. A visit to the seashore on a sunny day may be just the thing to cure the winter blues. The adjacent photograph was taken at Donkersley Beach on a glorious day in February.

VIVIAN ISLAND
Georgia Strait

It's a matter of being in the right place at the right time. Vivian Island, located just beyond Harwood Island in the Malaspina Strait, was labeled "Bare Rock" long ago. The uninviting name is understandable; for most of the year there is little to see on the small island apart from rocky landscape and shrunken vegetation. But there is a pigeonhole of time in spring and early summer when Vivian Island is a brilliant mass of wildflowers that delights all the senses.

As noted in *Powell River's First 50 Years*, the island's secret has been known for a long time. "If you care to go ashore on Vivian Island in early summer you will find yourself in an unbelievably lovely wonderland…The Snake Lily, London Pride, Star of Bethlehem, Larkspur, Musk, Wild Rose, Tiger Lily and alpine blossoms which spread a gorgeous perfume, are abundant in all directions." The adjacent photo shows Seablush in full bloom in April. Sadly, the beauty is short-lived. "There is no water on Vivian Island, the flowers and other growth are fed by the dew and the early rainfall. But in the summertime the hot sun blazes down on the island unchecked and undimmed. In a few days, almost, it seems, in a few hours, the floral loveliness disappears. In a minute flicker of time it dries up and fades away. Nothing remains but dry and withered growth."

There are a great number of small islands to explore in the Upper Sunshine Coast area, but Vivian has some small fame in the boating community. Because of its desert-like microclimate, prickly cacti grow there. This unusual island is home to a colony of sea lions, as well as a number of birds including eagles, cormorants and oystercatchers (pictured below). Those lucky enough to experience Vivian during the brief window of opportunity when the island is virtually alive with colour, are reminded of the fragile beauty of life.

EAGLE (LOIS) RIVER
Stillwater

"Geronimo!"

The jubilant cry rings through the canyon at Eagle River on hot summer days. This swimming hole is a favoured hangout for people seeking relief from the sizzling sun, especially those looking for a thrill. There are many tales of adventure-seekers leaping off the cliffs at Eagle River and plunging into the deep pools below. But the area is not monitored and cliff jumping is not recommended; jumpers and swimmers use the area at their own risk.

Besides its beauty and recreational value, the river is historically significant. Locally, it is still known unofficially by its original name, Eagle River. It was so called because eagles used to fly through the canyons in search of salmon. A railway, started in 1908 by John O'Brien, Dwight Brooks and M. Joseph Scanlon to service their logging company, was named The Eagle River and Northern Railway. It ran parallel to Eagle River and operated out of Stillwater for forty-six years before the rails were removed and truck logging took over.

Eagle River is fed by a series of lakes, including Lois and Khartoum, and the Lois Dam regulates its force. It was renamed Lois River a few years before construction of the Lois River dam site commenced in 1931. First, a crib dam was built, along with a penstock, the Stillwater powerhouse, and a surge tank. In May 1940 the Powell River Company started work on a permanent concrete dam. That dam (raised 6 metres in 1947) is still in operation today. Because Eagle River is a working river, it is imperative that people using the canyon as a recreation area keep their ears open. Before the floodgates of the dam are opened, a siren is sounded in warning, and anyone near the river should move – quickly!

CALIFORNIA SEA LION

Zalophus californianus

One of the noisier aquatic mammals in the Upper Sunshine Coast area, the California Sea Lion can be easily recognized by its territorial bark, which sounds like a dog's. These animals are friendly and playful – they are what many people know as the "trained seal" of the circus and zoo. In the wild, sea lions indulge in play, tossing and catching various objects on their noses. When at sea they sometimes raft together, playing and jumping clear of the water's surface. They live in colonies; one male sea lion protects a harem of up to fifteen females. Males establish breeding territories, called rookeries, along the coast from May to July.

Adult male California Sea Lions grow up to 2.5 metres long and can weigh up to 380 kilograms. Females grow to 2 metres long and weigh up to 115 kilograms. Despite their impressive size, California Sea Lions are the fastest aquatic carnivore; they can swim up to 40 kilometres per hour. Their main food sources include squid, octopus, crab, abalone, and fish, and they sometimes dive as deep as 140 metres to find food. They can also move relatively quickly on land because their wing-like front flippers have a similar bone structure to a human's arms and hands. California Sea Lions can be found on the North American Pacific Coast, from southern British Columbia down to Baja California and the Galapagos Islands. Although they often live on islands, they also inhabit secluded stretches of rocky beach on the mainland.

California Sea Lions have a thick layer of blubber, short coarse fur, and a dog-like head. They have good eyesight, but no colour vision, and good hearing, despite their small ears. Sensitive whiskers enhance their sense of touch. Males often have a thick, furry mane encircling their necks. California Sea Lions were once killed in great numbers for their blubber, which was used to make oil, but today this species is protected by international laws.

EMMA LAKE
South Powell Divide

This gorgeous aqua-blue lake is situated 32 kilometres north of Powell River, up the Eldred River. It is located in alpine territory at approximately 1300 metres, and is the centre point of the South Powell Divide. It is accessible by hiking trail, float plane (during ice-free months) and helicopter. Emma Lake has been a favoured hiking destination among alpine enthusiasts since members of the local Alpine Club built the first trail to the location about twenty years ago. Like many lakes in the area, Emma was unofficially named by loggers, and the name was transferred to the first maps that were made of the back country. The woman who was presumably its namesake remains a mystery.

Around 1989 the Powell River Forest Service built a public-use cabin at the lake. It was meant to be the first of three cabins, but it is the only one that has been built along the South Powell Divide to the present date. Today the cabin is user-maintained, and is mostly visited in the summer and fall months. In the deep of winter, the cabin is often buried; only a pole protruding from the roof betrays its presence. Nevertheless, some adventurous and experienced hikers do venture in each winter, and the cabin is accessible through an upper window. Emma Lake usually thaws by late July and freezes again by the end of November.

BALD EAGLE
Haliaeetus leucocephalus

Majestic and stately, the bald eagle keeps watch over the coastline, and as it soars through the air, people stop and look up. It is a bird that demands attention and garners respect. As its powerful wings carry it from one treetop to another, spectators sense the privilege of a special moment.

An adult bald eagle can have a wingspan up to 2.5 metres, and is easily recognized by its snow-white head, yellow, hooked bill, and brownish-black body. The name "bald" is derived from the Old English word "balde," which means white; the eagle was named for its white feathers rather than a lack of feathers. One eagle has about seven thousand feathers. The females are usually about thirty per cent larger than the males. They build enormous nests at the top of large trees, and often use the same nest year after year.

Primarily fish eaters, bald eagles pluck their dinner from the water with knife-like talons. They can fly 35 to 65 kilometres per hour and dive through the air at speeds faster than 160 kilometres per hour. They also hunt and scavenge small mammals, snakes, and other birds.

Bald eagles are frequently spotted as one is driving along Highway 101 from Saltery Bay, right out to Lund. However, the presence of such a magnificent bird should not be taken for granted. At one time bald eagles could be found throughout North America, but as a result of hunting, poaching and the encroachment of civilization, today they are only common in the rainforest coasts of Alaska and northern and central British Columbia.

SCUBA DIVING
Mermaid Cove

Those who descend into the depths of another world find that the beauty of the Upper Sunshine Coast extends far beyond the surface of the ocean. Clear and sheltered waters have made Powell River famous as one of the primary diving destinations in the world. There is a whole spectrum of colourful aquatic life to observe, from sea cucumbers and rock scallops to wolf-eels, giant pacific octopi and harbour seals.

Winter is a particularly good time to dive in the area, with visibility up to 30 metres. More than one hundred unique sites attract divers to Powell River; perhaps the most famous is the 2.5-metre bronze mermaid sculpture that is anchored in 18 metres of water offshore from Saltery Bay Provincial Park. Another well-known attraction is the floating breakwater of ten concrete hulks at the local mill. The wreck of the *Malahat*, which lies beneath the waves just outside the log pond, makes an accessible and fascinating dive. There are also several natural wrecks of old sailing ships and sunken tugboats that provide refuge for marine life in deeper waters.

Scuba diving is a popular pastime among locals, as well as visitors. Over the years a number of clubs have been formed and dismantled, but there always remains a core group of enthusiasts, and they often gather for group dives, especially in unusual locations. Inquire at local dive shops for more information about diving in the area, or for rental equipment and lessons.

Parris Champoise has been photographing the BC Coast – above and below water – for more than twenty-five years. Although he lives and works in Victoria, Powell River is one of his favourite places to dive. Through his company, Visions of Parris, he sells limited edition prints of his photographs.

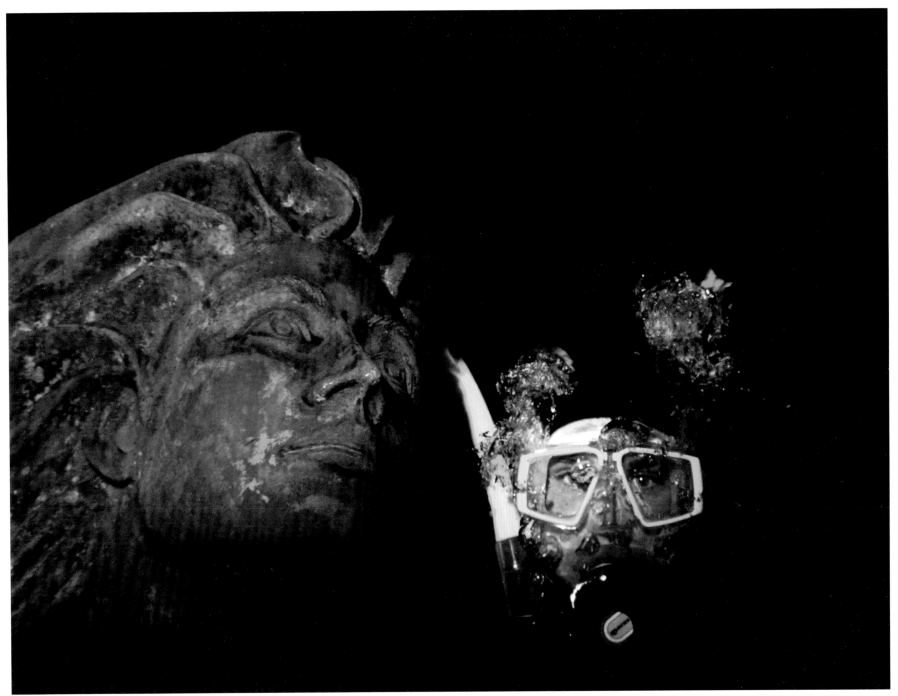

Photo by Parris Champoise

GARDENING
A Westview Garden

A cup of sun, a tablespoon of rain, and a pinch of fertile soil. The essential ingredients for a magnificent garden are found all along the Upper Sunshine Coast. From February to October, gardens boast the healthy glow and vibrant colours of a wide variety of flowers and greenery. First come winter jasmine, camellias and heather; followed by daffodils, forsythias and magnolias. Rhododendrons and azaleas are not far behind; then lilacs, wisteria, peonies and irises start to bloom. By summer the air is filled with the fragrance of oriental lilies. Daylilies, honeysuckle, and delphiniums rule the season. Roses and hydrangeas often last through the summer and into the golden warmth of autumn.

This area is heaven for those who love gardening, and they gather – formally and informally – to share ideas, seeds, and plants. The Powell River Garden Club started in 1967, and now boasts about eighty members. Flowers seem to be everywhere during the summer, and the garden club helps contribute to that feeling. The active membership holds a plant sale every May, and a flower show in July.

Beautiful flower gardens are easily seen in many people's front yards, but a peek into backyards around town can be another treat entirely. Fabulous gardens are often hiding in the most unusual places. The Powell River Spring Garden Tour gives locals and visitors the opportunity to explore private gardens. With the money that is raised, the tour committee supports local beautification and green-space projects.

It is not only flowers that are plentiful in the Powell River area. Thanks to a long growing season and diverse microclimates, many people grow a wide assortment of fruits and vegetables. Powell River is a designated GMO (Genetically Modified Organisms) Free zone, and fresh, local produce is readily available for much of the year. The Open Air Market in Padgett Valley is a great place to shop for fruit, vegetables and flowers in summer months.

CANOEING
Powell Forest Canoe Route

Water rippling, paddles dipping, muscles stretching. Canoeing is an obvious form of recreation in an area blessed with so many pristine lakes. One way to really enjoy the wilderness of the Upper Sunshine Coast is to pack a canoe and some supplies and head out to the Powell Forest Canoe Route.

The canoe route is 90 kilometres long, and weaves its way through eight lakes and five well-marked-and-maintained portages. It starts at Lois Lake and winds up and around through Horseshoe, Nanton, Ireland, Dodd, Windsor, Goat, and Powell lakes (see the map on page 3). The journey, which takes paddlers through protected waterways and impressive forest reserves, can be completed at a relaxed pace in five days. There are more than twenty campsites and canoe rest stops along the route, and all of the lakes are accessible by logging road. The best time to do the canoe route is June through October, when the weather is fairly reliable; it is a good idea to consult local outdoor stores for advice about conditions.

The Powell Forest Canoe Route is now being used as the setting for an organized event. In August 2004 the first annual Great Canadian Canoe Race took place. The competition, which challenges participants to complete the entire route in two days, brings together the tradition of wilderness exploration by canoe in Canada and the challenges of competition and physical endurance. Visit the race website www.greatcanadiancanoe.ca for more information.

Canoeists looking for variety will not be disappointed. Besides the canoe route, there are many other lakes and sheltered coastline areas to explore. An exciting physical challenge, or a peaceful weekend paddle: there is a lake and a piece of paradise for everyone.

LOIS LAKE
Stillwater

At one time Powell River was known for having the largest pulp and paper mill in the world. One of the things that made the mill successful was the abundance of hydroelectric power generated by its two dams. When the mill was built in the early 1900s, it depended solely on power from the Powell River Dam. In the 1930s the development of a second dam began in Stillwater and the Lois Lake reservoir, located about 24 kilometres east of Powell River, was created.

The Lois River Dam confined the waters of the first two Gordon Pasha Lakes. Lois Weaver, who was general manager of the Brooks Scanlon & O'Brien Logging Company at Stillwater, named the resulting reservoir (and Lois River) after himself. Lois Lake is about 14 kilometres long, and it is connected to Khartoum Lake (formerly the third Gordon Pasha Lake) by a channel. The dam and its powerhouse at Stillwater still provide energy to the mill today.

Lois Lake has a ghostly beauty about it; hundreds of dead tree spikes rise from the water and tell the story of a forest now gone. For many years it has been a popular recreation site. Despite potential hazards due to submerged stumps, it is known as a good location for freshwater fishing. It is part of the Powell Forest Canoe Route, and has a recreation site with nine campgrounds on its south side. Recently, Lois Lake has been recognized for another reason. An underwater timber harvesting operation has been removing logs from the flooded forests in the lake, and the innovative project has received a good deal of media attention.

HIKING
Appleton Creek Trail

Wooded areas blanket the Upper Sunshine Coast, and the extensive trail system that winds through them create a hiker's paradise. An intricate web connects various parts of the town of Powell River, as well as the regions around town. With enough time and energy, a person could get almost anywhere they needed to go on the trails!

Old, grown-over logging roads and old rail grades are the source of many trails. In addition, numerous paths have been fashioned by hiking and biking enthusiasts. There are already enough established trails to keep hikers on their toes year-round, but new trails often spring up – created by locals looking for a new challenge, or access to a new area. Some of the coast's best-known trails exist in the Duck Lake area – Lang Creek, Sweetwater, and Suicide Creek to name a few. There are several good hikes right out of Powell River, like Valentine Mountain, Scout Mountain, and Willingdon Beach. North of town the Marathon Trail, Dinner Rock, and Appleton Creek are examples of enjoyable hikes, each with their own highlights. In addition, there are many beautiful hikes on Texada and Savary islands.

Individuals and organized groups play an important role in maintaining trails. The BOMB (Bloody Old Men's Brigade) Squad is a troop of retired men who have worked together to maintain, reroute, and create trails since 1989. They have built more than sixty bridges, which make difficult or dangerous trail sections easier to navigate. The adjacent photograph shows a BOMB Squad bridge on the Appleton Creek Trail, built in 2005.

With so much variety and beauty to enjoy, it is little wonder that hiking is such a widespread hobby in the area. There are several annual hiking events, and the Powell River Hiking Club organizes hikes twice a week. To find out more, contact the Visitor's Information Centre on Marine Avenue.

SUNSETS

Myrtle Rocks

Breathtaking sunsets are a year-round phenomenon on the Upper Sunshine Coast. It is not uncommon to see people stopped by the side of the road, looking out at the ocean and the falling sun with an air of reverence. Shades of red, orange and purple reach across the sky, reminding those lucky enough to live in or visit Powell River to take time to stop and appreciate the splendour.

One of the best places to watch the sun go down is at a clear stretch of road along the highway, about 5 kilometres south of Powell River, known as Myrtle Rocks. Not only is the view spectacular, it was one of the early areas to be settled along this part of the coast. First, it was inhabited by local Coast Salish peoples. Then, in the late 1800s, a man by the name of Frolander bought 48 hectares of waterfront that became known as Myrtle Point. The area was named after a daughter of the McCormick family who was among the first to put down roots there. Frolander ran a post office, did some logging on the land, and then sold it (and an additional 48 hectares which spread back to Paradise Valley) to the company Bloedel, Welch and Stewart for use as a logging location and booming ground.

A community grew up at Myrtle Point, but for a while no wharf existed there. As a result, the Union Steamship, the Comox, dropped freight and passengers on an anchored float offshore and travellers had to wait for a boat to pick them up. Sometime between 1911 and 1917 a wharf was built at Myrtle Rocks, the pilings of which can still be seen today. The pilings, in their stunning setting, are one of the most commonly photographed scenes in the Powell River area, especially when there's a beautiful sunset.

Thank you to these local sponsors who have made this book possible.

Thank you to these local sponsors who have made this book possible.

The idea to produce a book like *Off the Beaten Path* has been in the works for several years. Anyone who has lived in or visited Powell River knows what an incredibly beautiful place it is, and yet until now there has never been a book that focuses solely on the Upper Sunshine Coast, showcasing its strengths and treasures. Sisters Emma Levez Larocque and Tara Chernoff decided to combine their skills to produce such a book and get it out to the public. This has truly been a combined effort between them, and it would not have been possible without the financial support of various businesses and organizations listed.

Tara Chernoff has spent time traveling both within Canada and around the world. She and her husband chose Powell River as the place to raise their family not only for its extraordinary beauty, but also the wide variety of activities available in their backyard. "Powell River is our playground – we love it here." Tara has more than ten years of professional sales and marketing experience. Her background, combined with her love of Powell River, made the opportunity to do the sales and marketing for this book a perfect fit.

Emma Levez Larocque has lived and worked in Powell River for seven years. Having spent much of her life in Ontario, she appreciates – every day – the natural beauty of the coast. Emma has been taking photographs since she was ten years old, and remembers discovering an amazing new world when her father gave her his Canon A-1. "Taking pictures is like looking at the world through the eyes of a child – always new, always exciting."

Thanks to contributing photographers Lorrie Pirart, Parris Champoise, as well as the Powell River Academy of Music.

Writing and photography is a natural combination, and Emma has been writing professionally for about ten years. She has authored *People of the White City, stories from the Powell River Mill*, and co-authored *Many Voices: Music and the Arts in Powell River*.

Abby-Gail J. Hyldig has been painting and wood-carving since she was old enough to hold a pencil. Abby studied at the Kootenay School of the Arts in Nelson, BC. Through her company, Crabby Abby Art, she does a variety of artwork, including painting, carving, jewellery, pottery, and textiles. She lives in Powell River and can sometimes be seen at local events, like Art in the Park, displaying her work.